# the BOOK of MeNTaLism

by Tom Mason and Dan Danko
with John Railing and Danny Orleans, Professional Magicians

Scholastic Inc.
New York • Toronto • London • Auckland • Sydney
Mexico City • New Delhi • Hong Kong • Buenos Aires

ISBN 0-439-32703-2

Copyright © 2001 by Scholastic Inc.

Design by Mark Neston
Illustrations by Daniel Aycock

12 11 10 9 8 7 6 5                    2 3 4 5 6/0

Printed in the U.S.A.

First Scholastic printing, November 2001

# tABLe of CONTENts

# the magic of mentalism

**"I'm thinking of a number..."**

Can you guess what someone is thinking? Can you predict the future? Do you have X-ray vision or extrasensory perception (ESP)?

This month, you'll learn how to create a special type of magic...the magic that lets you read minds.

Magicians call this kind of thing *mental magic* or *mentalism*. And as you might have guessed, magicians who specialize in mental tricks are called *mentalists*.

How can you see colors hidden inside a black box? Or know the number on a die that your friend has picked? How can you predict choices someone hasn't even made yet?

*Our* prediction is that you'll find out how in this book! As you learn these mentalism tricks, practice them regularly, and create your own patter, you'll be able to create your own mentalism show, like many of the great mentalists who have preceded you.

Way back in the late 1800s, Anna Eva Fay and her husband, Henry, did a two-person mind-reading act. Their son John and his wife, Eva, carried on the great family tradition with a more high-powered act of their own. Eva called herself the "High Priestess of Mysticism." They put on a huge show with fantastic robes, fancy turbans, and ornate costumes. People came from miles away to see these "all-powerful" mind readers!

And just what does that have to do with Magic University? Glad you asked! Many of the mentalism tricks you'll learn this month are based on the tricky techniques that were used by the Fays and other great mentalists of the 20th century.

Probably the most famous mentalist working today is the Israeli wonder worker, Uri Geller, who claims that he really has psychic powers. He bends spoons and keys with his mind, makes seeds grow right in his hands, and starts broken watches by gently rubbing them. Though most magicians believe that he is a fake, lots of people have paid him to use his psychic abilities to find oil and do biological research.

That's enough on the history of mentalism! Now it's time for you to learn the secrets and techniques of the world's greatest mentalists. You'll learn how to pretend to have X-ray vision, what to do when a prediction trick doesn't work, and how to read secret markings on playing cards. (But here's a word of caution: Once you do that last trick, even your best friends will never play cards with you again!)

After you've practiced and mastered working with the props from your MENTALISM KIT, your friends will be asking, "Can you really read minds?" You can tell them that you went to Magic University, or better yet, you can tell them what Sidney Piddington told his radio audiences when his wife correctly guessed a word that was chosen from a book miles from where she was standing: "Real or fake? You be the judge!"

So crack your knuckles, flex your fingers, and more important, open your mind. You're about to enter the exciting world of mentalism!

**P. S.** If you riffle the lower right-hand corner of all the pages in this book, you'll see something that will totally *flip* you out!

## assignment: Guess what color is hidden inside a box!

## box of color

If you can tell the difference between red and green, not only can you tell the difference between an apple and a piece of broccoli, you can do this trick, too. By creating the illusion that you placed the box lid on top of the box when in fact you placed it on the side, you're able to see the color hidden inside. How do you put a lid on the side of a box and make people think it's really the top? Read on!

## magic must-haves: Magic trunk

## from your mentalism kit:
Multi-colored cube; box and lid

## extras:
A volunteer who doesn't know the trick

## backstage
Nothing for you to do this time!

## show time!

*"One thing that many people don't realize is that color emits heat. We've all heard of hot pink, fire red, or cool blue. Because colors do emit heat, it's easy to figure out a color without looking—if you know the temperature for each."*

**STEP 1:** Show the audience the multi-colored cube and the box and lid. Let them touch the cube, box, and lid. They can rub them, lick them, anything to prove to themselves that these items are the real deal. No trapdoors, no hidden rabbits. Then pick a volunteer.

*"As you can see, the six-sided cube has a different color on each side. Careful! The red side gets hot! I'll turn my back and I want you to put the cube in the box with the color you selected facing up. Then stick the lid on the box and be sure to close it up tight!"*

**STEP 2:** Turn your back and wait. If your volunteer does decide to lick the cube to see if it's real, you may want to ask her or him to wipe it off before putting it back in the box. Once the color has been selected, have the person place the covered box in your hand.

**STEP 3:** This is the tricky part. Keep both hands behind you and, while the audience is distracted by your turning to face them, move the lid of the box to one of the

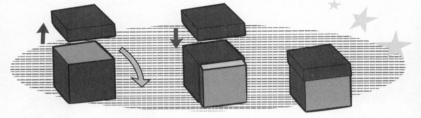

sides of the box. Now turn the entire box so that the side of the box with the lid is on top. This will make it look as if it really *is* the top of the box.

> **Trick Tip:** It's a good idea to speak to the audience while you flip the box lid to one of the sides. It will help cover any noise you make as you move the lid.

*"Now it's just a simple act of feeling the temperature at the top of the box, which will instantly tell me the color of the chosen side of the cube."*

**STEP 4:** Bring the box in front of you. The open part of the box should face you at all times. Make sure no one can see the opening—the audience must think that the box is still closed.

Casually glance at the open box—and the cube inside—to see the color the volunteer selected. Don't stare and gawk like you just spotted your favorite celebrity at the Burger Barn! Let's say that the color is green. You could then say something like this:

*"I'm getting something. It's something warm and alive...like it's growing...."*

**STEP 5:** Milk it! Don't just yell out the color. Take a few moments to work into it. Maybe tap the box, or touch a thermometer to it. Really get into the showmanship of the moment and entertain the audience. Then finally announce your "guess."

*"...Growing like a plant...or a tree. A green tree. It's green! Right?"*

**STEP 6:** This is the next tricky part. As you say **"Right?"** look the audience in the eye, so they're watching you, not the box. At the same time, lift the lid of the box with your right hand and rotate the box one-quarter turn with your left hand. Show the audience the color cube and reveal you were correct. It's green!

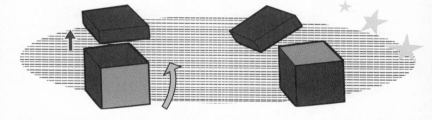

**Trick Tip:** This last move is a doozy. If you don't feel up to the task, simply move the box to behind your back, rotate the lid to the real top of the box, bring the box to the front again, place it on the magic trunk, and reveal the cube.

## HOMEWORK:

Practice steps 4 and 6. It's important that these are done naturally and quietly. You don't want the audience to hear you move the plastic lid around and it's always a bad idea to say, **"Okay, now this is the part of the trick where I need everyone to plug their ears."**

**LESSON:** Use symbol cards to make a prediction!

## COUNTDOWN

We hate to break some bad news to you, but you don't actually make any real predictions here. The placement of the preselected card is the key to allowing you to predict the same card every time!

## FROM YOUR MENTALISM KIT:

Six symbol cards

## HOMEMADE MAGIC:
Table, pencil, paper, and an envelope (Don't worry, you won't be writing a letter to Aunt Petunia.)

## EXTRAS:
One volunteer who doesn't know the trick

## BACKSTAGE

Before you begin, draw a square (that's the shape with four equal sides) on a piece of paper. Put this in an envelope and seal it up. If you hate licking envelopes, take a small sticky note and stick it to the back of the card with the square and write, **"You will select the square."**

## SHOW TIME!

*"I've been working real hard to develop my ability to see into the future. At first I could only see two seconds into the future, but that wasn't very helpful. By the time I tried to tell someone what was going to happen, it already had."*

**STEP 1:** Deal out the six symbol cards onto the table. Starting from the left, the square must be in the fourth position.

"But recently, I've been able to stretch my ability to see into the future a full five minutes."

**STEP 2:** Select your volunteer. Make sure it's someone who won't faint when he witnesses this amazing trick. That's always embarrassing. And if he *does* faint, just yell out **"Ta-da! And I hypnotized him, too!"**

Have your volunteer think of a number from one to six.

**"Got your number? Do you want to change your mind?"**

No matter how he responds, add, **"I already knew that."** It gets a good laugh.

**"Okay, if you don't want to change your mind again, tell me your number."**

**STEP 3:** For this example, let's say the volunteer picked five. Starting with the card on your left, spell out F-I-V-E. This will land you on the square.

---

**Trick Tip:** This is a *force*—no matter what number the volunteer picks, you'll always land on the square. Say what?! Just check out this nifty list below to see what we mean. When the volunteer chooses:
One, start at the first card on your *right* and spell O-N-E.
Two, start at the first card on your *right* and spell T-W-O.
Three, start at the first card on your *right* and count 1-2-3.
Four, start at the first card on your *left* and count 1-2-3-4.
Five, start at the first card on your *left* and spell F-I-V-E.
Six, start at the first card on your *right* and spell S-I-X.

---

**"Ah, the square! One of my favorite shapes! And to prove that it is, I made a little prediction about it...."**

**STEP 4:** Have the volunteer tear open the envelope and remove the piece of paper inside, revealing the square! (Or, if you used a sticky note, have him turn over the square card, revealing the note on the back.)

"*I can't wait to go to Las Vegas.*"

## HOMEWORK:

Remember the counting method. That's it. Nothing else. Nice, huh?

**Trick Tip:** You can use any symbol card you want as the predicted shape. Just make sure this card is in the fourth position from the left.

## RHINE NOT?

Special cards with symbols, similar to the kind you used in this trick, were designed at the Parapsychology Laboratory at Duke University to test *extrasensory perception,* or *ESP*. They are sometimes called *Rhine Cards* because Dr. Joseph Rhine founded the laboratory in 1934.

# aLL-seeiNG eye #3

**pRojeCt:** Predict the shapes a volunteer will draw!

## sHape-sHifteR

Relying on the fact that a majority of people choose the same shape when asked to draw a simple geometric figure, you're able to pre-select the symbol cards to match their drawing.

**maGic must-HaVes:** Magic trunk

**fRom youR meNtaLism kit:** Symbol cards

**HomemaDe maGic:** Pencil, paper, and tall glass of cool lemonade

**extRas:** One volunteer who knows how to draw a straight line (but doesn't know the trick)

## backstaGe

Take a sip of the lemonade.

## sHow time!

*"What would you say if I told you I could read your mind?"*

Wait for the audience's response, then add, *"I know what you're thinking...really. And to prove it, I'm going to conduct a little experiment."*

**STEP 1:** Choose a volunteer, and give him the pencil and paper. Pull out the circle and triangle cards and place them facedown on the magic trunk. They're your prediction!

*"I want you to draw something. Make sure I can't see what you're doing. I want you to draw a simple geometric figure—something like a square."*

**STEP 2:** Watch the movement of the pencil. Even though you can't see what he's drawing, if you watch the pencil,

you should have a pretty
good idea.

*"Done? Good. Now I
want you to draw
a second simple
geometric figure, also
something like a square,
inside the first one."*

**Trick Tip:** Make sure you say the exact same phrases:
*"simple geometric figure"* and *"like a square."* Why? Because
these phrases limit the volunteer's choices. There are not
many simple geometric figures, and by adding *"like a
square,"* most people will not draw a square as a result.
Tricky!

**STEP 3:** Watch the movement of the pencil. Again, this
may tip you off to what he's drawing.

**STEP 4:** Once the volunteer finishes, ask him to put
down the pencil and concentrate on the shapes he's
drawn. Now it's time for you to use your information.
Having watched the pencil's movements, do you think
the volunteer chose something other than a circle and
triangle?

This is the only tricky part and the place where things
can get goofed up.

If you think the volunteer drew something other than
a circle and triangle, ignore the two symbol cards and
announce your guess. Make sure you're certain! This is
where the tall glass of cool lemonade can come in
handy, 'cause don't be surprised if you're sweating at
this step!

However, if you couldn't tell what shapes he chose, or
suspect they are a circle and triangle, then motion to
the symbol cards.

*"Before you even started drawing, I saw the images in your brain and made a prediction! Do you think I'm right?"*

**STEP 5:** Slowly, dramatically, flip over the first card, then the second card and have the volunteer reveal his drawing.

**STEP 6:** If your prediction turns out to be wrong, now's the time for a clever story—or a quick escape! Try saying something like, **"See, I predicted what shapes you *wouldn't* draw!"**

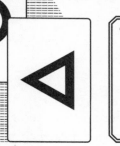

> **Trick Tip:** 80% of the people draw a circle inside a triangle and most of the rest draw a triangle inside a circle. How do we know this? Years and years of government study and testing.

HOMEWORK: Have a friend draw shapes while you watch the pencil movement to see if you can identify the shapes. If you can master this, you'll rule the world! (Or maybe just impress some people with magic.)

EXTRA CREDIT: To add a twist to this trick, forget the symbol cards, and make your own drawing as the volunteer makes his. Whether you go with the odds and draw the triangle/circle combo or try to guess what he's drawing from the pencil movements, it's a neat twist to reveal the two drawings at the same time.

EXTRA-EXTRA CREDIT: For a really cool glass of lemonade, add more ice cubes.

**LESSON:** Name the card a volunteer has chosen!

## LINE BY LINE

Check out how the symbol cards can be arranged in an easily remembered order—according to the number of lines or sides in each figure:

Circle—one continuous line

Plus—two crossed lines

Triangle—three lines

Square—four lines or sides

Star—five points

Hexagon—six sides

Once you've memorized this order and stacked the cards this way, you'll always know what card comes before any other card in the sequence, and this will let you figure out what card your volunteer has picked!

## MAGIC MUST-HAVES: Magic trunk

## FROM YOUR MENTALISM KIT: Symbol cards

## EXTRAS: One volunteer who doesn't know the trick

## BACKSTAGE

Stack the cards facedown in the following order: circle, plus, triangle, square, star, hexagon.

## SHOW time!

*"As you may not know, I'm studying to become a mind reader. I can't do anything really complicated yet, like figure out what my teacher's going to put on tomorrow's test, but if you think of a shape, I bet I can pick it right out of your brain."*

**STEP 1:** Place the stack of cards on the magic trunk and have a volunteer *cut,* not shuffle, the cards. (That means he should divide the deck into two piles, and put the bottom pile on the top. Let him cut the cards as many times as he wants, but don't let him cut the deck for too long. Watching someone cut cards is really boring!)

*"Okay. Enough already. Pick up the top card and look at it, but don't show it to me! Concentrate really hard on the shape pictured on the card."*

**STEP 2:** As your volunteer picks up the top card, remove the remainder of the stack from the trunk, but take a quick peek at the bottom card. This will reveal the identity of the card the volunteer picked off the top. How? Easy!

Regardless of how many times the volunteer cut the deck, the overall card sequence is the same: circle, plus, triangle, square, star, hexagon. (That's why you didn't want him to shuffle the cards—it would have messed up the order.) If the card on the bottom is the triangle, he picked the square. Is the bottom card the star? Then he picked the hexagon. See? It's the same order! Cutting the deck only changed where the sequence began, but not the sequence itself.

"*Your mind's pretty easy to read. Are you sure there's anything else in there? I'm getting a clear picture of a... [name the card].*"

HOMEWORK: Make sure you've memorized that card order!

---

**PLANET OF THE (MAGIC) APES**

Originally known as the "Bad Boys of Magic," Penn Jillette and Teller (he doesn't have a first name) first became famous in the 1980s when they started performing their own wacky style of magic in the United States. One of their routines involves a strange character named Mofo the Psychic Gorilla. The audience sees what looks like a real head of a gorilla (with no body attached) hooked up to various medical devices in an effort to keep it alive. The gorilla head appears to talk and can tell audience members the names of cards they picked and serial numbers on dollar bills from their pockets!

---

# Secrets of the marked deck:

## tricks 5 & 6

Lucky you. The deck of cards you got in this kit is *marked* and *tapered*.

So what, you say? We'll let you in on a little secret: Marked and Tapered are not two brothers from Greece. A marked and tapered deck is a deck of playing cards that looks absolutely normal to the untrained eye. But *we're* training your eye—and your fingers—so, get ready to start learning the secrets of the ultimate gimmicked card deck. We'll start with the *marked* part. You'll find out about the *tapered* thing on page 25.

Marked cards use a code—special secret markings on the back of each card. This means you can identify any card by looking at the markings and comparing it to the special *key* that you've memorized. The *key* clues you in to the code on the card back and tells you what each card is. Go ahead, take a look at the cards now. Do you see the code on each card back? No? Good! That means no one else will, either.

But with practice, you can read the code and know exactly which card is which. Check it out! In the upper left corner on the back of each card is a special notation: A line through one of the dots. Look at the key on this page, and you'll see that the angle of the line through the dot tells you whether the card is a spade, heart, diamond or club. Where that line appears also tells you the rank of the card. Look at the key again and

**Marked Card Key**

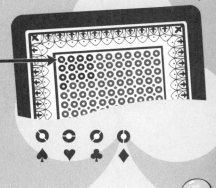

17

you'll see that starting from the very top left corner, the cards are marked in reverse count order: king, queen, jack, ten, nine, etc.

Once you find the mark and match it to its position, you'll know the card and the suit. We've put some examples on the next page, so you can see what we mean. And if you wear glasses, don't forget 'em! Eyesight is the key here!

Reading marked cards is not easy and requires a lot of practice. Nothing will ruin the trick quicker than a magician squinting and staring at the back of a card while doing a trick—and you can't bring the key onstage with you, either! One way to practice is to deal the cards slowly and read the code as you deal. See if you can pick specific cards and then find them in the deck. Or find all four aces, all four kings, all four queens, etc. The more you practice, the more natural it will appear to the audience. But you knew that already, right?

But there's more to using a marked deck than knowing the code and the key, however. If you have a volunteer pick a card and you just call out what it is, you'll tip off the audience. The point of magic isn't just to do the impossible. The point is to *amaze* people that you can do the impossible.

Keeping this in mind, here are some simple guidelines to doing tricks with marked decks:

- **Don't cluster tricks requiring a marked deck together.** Like making a salad, mix it up, man! If you do three or four marked card tricks in a row, it's easier for the audience to catch on, especially if you are squinting and staring at the card backs. Did we already mention this was a bad thing to do?

- **Learn to read the cards with a glimpse and always make up an excuse to look at the card.** One good way is to place it on the top of the deck and ask the volunteer to touch it. This ordinary diversion will give you a reason to look at the card, which will shift any possible suspicion. Or create your own way to check out the markings on the back of the card. Yelling, **"Oh, my gosh! Aliens!"** and then checking out the back of the card while everyone else looks the other way may seem like a good diversion, but trust us, it's not. Funny, yes. Good diversion, no.

- **Use your imagination.** Don't just reveal a card by saying, **"And here's your card."** That's like eating plain oatmeal: B-O-R-I-N-G! Create fun ways to reveal the card: Draw a picture of it, read a mind, close your eyes and "feel" for the card, or whatever. Throw in some drama. Pretend you're struggling. Read a mind or two. Whatever! Just make it a show!

## Examples of Marked Cards

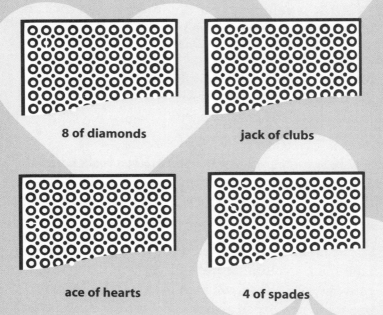

8 of diamonds

jack of clubs

ace of hearts

4 of spades

# tHUMBS-UP! #5

## PROJECT:
Guess a volunteer's card by spotting her thumbprint!

## CHECK FOR PRINTS
Ever want to be a detective? Now's your chance. You won't really be able to see your volunteer's thumbprint on the front of the card, but you *will* be able to read the secret key that tips you off to the card's identity.

## MAGIC MUST-HAVES: Magic trunk

## FROM YOUR MENTALISM KIT: Marked cards

## HOMEMADE MAGIC: A glass or any shiny article
(like a mirror)

## EXTRAS: A volunteer who doesn't know the trick and has at least one finger (ha, ha)

## BACKSTAGE
Make sure you've memorized the code and the key to the marked cards. If you have, then sit back and relax! If not, check out page 17 again.

## SHOW TIME!
*"I've been reading a lot of Sherlock Holmes books lately. It's amazing, the stuff you can learn from reading those books. One thing I picked up is how to spot a person's fingerprints at a crime scene."*

**STEP 1:** Take out the marked deck and place it on the table. Pick a volunteer and ask her to pull out a single card and lay it facedown next to the deck. This is a good opportunity to glance at the card back and check the markings that tell which card it is. Remember, no staring or drooling!

*"Now, I want you to 'steal' that card!"*

**STEP 2:** Instruct the volunteer to pick up the card and press her thumbprint against the face of the card.

*"But don't damage the card! These cost money, you know!"*

**STEP 3:** Have the volunteer slip the card back into the deck and then shuffle it to her heart's content.

**STEP 4:** Pull out the glass or shiny object and hand it to the volunteer. Ask her to touch it with her thumb.

*"But not too hard. I don't want you smudging the prints."*

**STEP 5:** Inspect the object that has the volunteer's thumbprint. Now is a good time to stare and squint as you examine the print.

*"Nice swirl pattern. Good loops and stuff. This'll be a piece of cake."*

**STEP 6:** Flip the deck faceup and start riffling through the cards. Occasionally pick out a card you know isn't the right one and "compare" it to the volunteer's prints on the shiny object. When you finally get to the volunteer's card, go past it a few cards, then stop.

*"Wait a second..."*

Go back to her card and pull it out. Hold it up next to the fingerprinted object.

*"I do believe I have found the stolen card and identified the culprit!"*

Then smile and quote the famous Sherlock Holmes line: *"Elementary, my dear Watson. Elementary."*

HOMEWORK: You guessed it. Practice checking the card markings in a casual and natural manner.

# card key

**assignment:** Guess a volunteer's card by feeling his pulse!

## beyond suspicion

Let's face it, if you keep doing amazing tricks guessing people's cards, someone will eventually accuse you of using marked cards. If you can't throw him or her out of your magic show, use this trick to prove that person wrong. By using the marks on the card that sits on the top of the deck, you'll be able to know which card was selected by the volunteer and placed on top of your card.

**magic must-haves:** Magic trunk

**from your mentalism kit:** Marked cards

**extras:** One volunteer who doesn't know the trick

## backstage

Got that code and key to the marked cards memorized? Okay, then we'll stop bugging you about it! If you haven't, then check out page 17 again.

## show time!

*"Many people don't realize that a lot of magicians' tricks are really just a good magician being able to 'read' the responses of their victim—I mean, volunteer."*

**STEP 1:** Place the deck on the table and ask the volunteer to shuffle it. Once he's done, note the top card by checking the markings on the back. Remember that card—that's your *key card*. Without it, you might as well be playing Go Fish.

**STEP 2:** Have the volunteer pull out a bunch of cards from the middle of the deck, *square* them (that is, even them up), and look at the card at the top of the pulled-out portion. Have him share it with the audience, but make sure the card's hidden from you. Now ask him to stick the card at the bottom of the pile of cards he's pulled out, and place this whole section on top of the entire deck like he's stacking a tomato on a ham sandwich. This puts your volunteer's card on top of your key card.

*"Remember your card. I guarantee you the next time you see it, your response will give its identity away."*

**STEP 3:** Cut, not shuffle, the deck a few times. You can have the volunteer do this as well, once you're feeling comfortable with this trick.

> **Trick Tip:** Your key card will always be below your volunteer's card. There's one exception: Your key card may end up on top of the deck. If so, don't worry. Your volunteer's card is therefore at the bottom of the deck.

**STEP 4:** Turn the deck faceup and spread the cards out so that the top card of the faceup deck is pushed toward your right and you can see all of them, or at least your key card and the one to the left of it—that's the card your volunteer picked! Remember: If your key card is the last card on the left (the top of the facedown deck) your volunteer's card is the card all the way to the right! Clear? Take your volunteer by his wrist and place your thumb so you can feel his pulse. You don't really need to feel his pulse, so pretend if you can't. Although, if he doesn't have a pulse, he's more amazing than this trick!

*"I want you to extend your finger like you're pointing and I'm going to slowly move your hand along the cards. The moment you pass over your card, your pulse will speed up and give you away!"*

**STEP 5:** Move his hand along the cards. As you reach the key card, keep going, passing over his selected card. This will trick the audience into thinking you goofed up, and in case you haven't guessed, tricking the audience is fun!

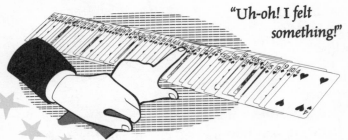

*"Uh-oh! I felt something!"*

Quickly move his hand back in the direction of his card and stop directly over it. Reveal the card with a flourish.

*"I hope you never have to take a lie detector test!"*

HomeWORK: Practice cutting the deck and making sure you keep the selected card next to the key card.

---

### I WANNA HOLD YOUR HAND (AND READ YOUR MIND)

In 1874, J. Randall Brown, a reporter for the Chicago *Inter-Ocean,* demonstrated some mind-reading tricks to his fellow reporters, claiming they were real. His abilities were so convincing that a medical college and Yale University tested him!

The secret behind his mind-reading stunts? A technique called *muscle reading.* Brown was the first person to discover that if you hold someone's hand, his or her grip can give you a lot of information about what he or she is thinking!

# Secrets of the tapered deck: tricks 7 & 8

As we said before, your deck of cards is also *tapered*, which means that the top of each card is slightly narrower than the bottom of each card. A tapered deck is also called a *stripper deck*. But that doesn't mean that you've got to undress the deck! To *strip* a deck means to hold your deck with the narrow half on top, and then turn one card around so that you can feel the edges of its wider half sticking out of the deck. This makes it really easy to get the card out of the deck. Once you've gotten the card out of the deck again, you've stripped it!

Still not sure what the heck we're talking about? Maybe you just need to feel it for yourself! Take any card from the tapered deck, spin it around (but don't turn it faceup), and slide it back into the deck. Feel how its edges protrude from the deck sides? Pretty sneaky, huh? Now, hold the deck in one hand, gripping it lightly by the sides, toward the bottom of the deck. Then slide the fingers of your other hand up the sides of the deck. See how your fingers move the reversed card out of the deck? You've stripped the deck!

You'll also notice that the sticking-out edges of the flipped card only appear on one end of the deck.

You must make sure you always strip in the direction of the flipped card's wider edge; otherwise, nothing will happen, except that your face will turn red from embarrassment.

You can do this little move with more than one card or even behind your back. Either way, it makes for an amazing effect! If you're using more than one reversed card, you may have to strip the deck a few times to get all of them, but don't worry! Just do it in a way that's mysterious to your audience and you'll wow them every time!

Also in the center of the back of each card is a graphic—a star with several different symbols. You only care about two of the pictures, the bottle and the lion. The bottle should always be at the top of the star and the lion at the bottom. When you start each tapered card trick, make sure that all of the cards are arranged in this way. If you flip a single card so that the lion is at the top, it's easy to find it in the deck, and it will come out when you strip the deck.

bottle

lion

**exercise:** Make a card magically rise from the deck!

## opposites attract

When you place the chosen card in the opposite direction from the rest of the deck, stripping it out is as easy as saying hocus-pocus! Actually, it's easier than saying hocus-pocus, as long as you've read *Secrets of the Tapered Deck* on pages 25–26 first.

**magic must-haves:** Magic trunk

**from your mentalism kit:** Tapered deck

**extras:** One volunteer who doesn't know the trick

## backstage

Not much. Just make absolutely certain all the cards in the tapered deck are facing the right way. This can be done by checking the bottle picture on the back of all the cards. Make sure that the bottle is at the top of the star for every card. You can also check the deck by feeling the sides. If they feel smooth, like a normal deck, you're good to go! This can be hard to do if too many cards are flipped, so double-check everything against the picture on the back of the deck!

## show time!

*"I've been told that I have a magnetic personality, but I didn't realize that people were really talking about my fingers!"*

**STEP 1:** Have a volunteer select a card from the deck and look at it, hiding its identity from you. She can show the audience if she wants to, just so long as you're not let in on the secret!

*"In fact, my fingers are so magnetic, they can even attract things that aren't metallic, like that card you hold."*

**STEP 2:** While the volunteer looks at the card or shows it to the audience, carefully turn the deck around to face the opposite direction. Make sure no one sees you do this! Now have the volunteer slip the card into the middle of the deck. Cut the deck as much as you want. The more you do, the more the audience will be satisfied the card is lost in the deck. If you're feeling adventurous, you can also ask your volunteer to cut the deck for you.

*"Now I'll take my magnetic fingers and pull the card from the deck."*

---

**Trick Tip:** Sometimes the volunteer will turn her card around, too. If she does, you shouldn't turn your deck around. Keep a close eye on the volunteer's card. Whether she turns her card or you turn your deck, you want to make certain they face in opposite directions.

---

**STEP 3:** Turn the deck so that the picture of the bottle on the back of the top card is at the top of the star picture. Hold the deck gently at the bottom with one hand and run your fingers up the edges. Your fingers will easily catch against the volunteer's card and magnetically make it rise from the deck!

**HOMEWORK:** Practice stripping the card from the deck. (Then brush your teeth! You can have fresh breath while doing magic, you know!)

**exercise:** Make four cards that are lost in the deck rise to the top!

## cream rises

And so do four selected cards in this trick. By stripping them out and placing them on top of the deck, it appears that they rose to the top!

**magic must-haves:** Magic trunk

**from your mentalism kit:** Tapered cards

**extras:** A volunteer who doesn't know the trick

## backstage

Not much. Just make absolutely certain all the cards in the tapered deck are facing the right way. This can be done by checking the bottle picture on the back of all the cards. Make sure that the bottle is at the top of the star of every card. Again, you can also do this by feel, making sure the tapered edges all line up and the sides of the deck feel smooth.

## show time!

*"Have you ever heard the story of the floating cards? No? That's because there's no such story, but after I show you this trick, there just might be!"*

**STEP 1:** Ask a volunteer to name a number or face card in the deck. For example, ace, nine, queen, four, etc. If the volunteer doesn't know the number and face cards in a deck, get a new volunteer! Has this guy been living under a rock or what? Let's say he chooses ace. Fan through the deck and pull out all the aces and lay them on the magic trunk.

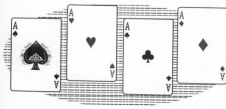

*"I'm going to take these four aces and lose them in the deck."*

**STEP 2:** Take the aces and slide them into different places within the deck. Square up the deck and cut it a few times until everyone is satisfied the cards are lost. You can even show them that the top card isn't an ace if you want.

> **Trick Tip:** Make sure that when you put the four cards in the deck they're in the opposite direction from the rest of the deck. You've got stripping to do!

*"Now, I'm going to place the cards behind my back [or under the table] and mix up all the cards without looking."*

**STEP 3:** Put the deck behind your back or under the table and strip out the four aces and place them on top of the deck. Do this as quickly and as quietly as possible.

**STEP 4:** Pull out the deck, and place it on the magic trunk. Flip over the top four cards, revealing the four aces.

*"Who says only cream rises to the top?"*

> **Trick Tip:** When it comes time to reveal the four cards on top of the deck, have the volunteer flip them over one at a time. Volunteers love to get involved...and who can blame them?

HOMEWORK: Practice stripping the four cards out of the deck without looking.

extra credit: Did you know there are entire books filled with tricks for marked and tapered cards? Honest. This isn't just a trick to get you into a library. You'll probably have better luck in a magic store, so check around to see if there's one in your area.

**assignment:** Use a crystal ball to magically see a card your friend has picked!

## Look into my crystal ball

It may not be crystal, but you do get a ball in your MENTALISM KIT, and it comes with a clear plastic shell that has a tiny card taped to the inside. You won't be able to use the card to play War or Spit, but it will be the same card your volunteer picked—and with magic, that's much more important!

## magic must-haves: Magic trunk

## from your mentalism kit: Crystal ball
and shell, marked and tapered deck of cards (actually, any deck will do)

## extras: A volunteer who doesn't know the trick

## backstage

Place the plastic shell in your pants pocket. It's best to wear loose or baggy pants for this trick. The grunge look may be out, but tight pants will reveal the plastic shell in your pocket. Then take the deck of cards, find the three of clubs, and place the card on top of the deck, facedown.

## show time!

"*Did you ever see The Wizard of Oz? Remember how the Wicked Witch of the West always watched Dorothy through her crystal ball? I guess that was before they had video cameras. Anyway, I thought it was pretty cool, so I went and found my own crystal ball.*"

**STEP 1:** Show the audience the clear ball. You can even toss it into the audience and let them touch it and see it up close.

*"I know what you're thinking. Why do I have a plastic, not a crystal, ball? Well, do you know how much real crystal costs? But trust me, this'll do just fine."*

**STEP 2:** Get the ball back from the audience and put it in your pocket. While you do this, distract the audience with your patter and slide the plastic shell over the ball. Now imagine how hard this would be to do in tight pants!

*"I'm going to need a volunteer to pick a card from this ordinary deck of cards; then, I'll use the not-so-crystal ball to see what it is."*

**STEP 3:** Show the audience the cards so they can be certain there's nothing sneaky going on, even though there *is* something sneaky going on. Place the deck facedown and prepare for a *Cross Cut Force*.

A *Cross Cut Force* is not what happens when your mom makes you share your french fries with your brother. Here's how it goes: Have a volunteer cut the deck once, making two piles of cards. Don't let him put the deck together again! You want to have two piles.

To assure the volunteer doesn't complete the cut, point to a spot on the magic trunk and say, **"Cut the deck and put half here."** If your volunteer is capable of following directions, you'll have two stacks.

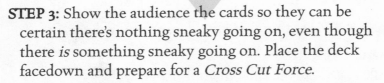

Now take the bottom portion of the deck

and place it crossways on top of what was the top portion of the deck. That's the *cross cut*! Remember, the bottom pile (which used to be at the top) has the three of clubs on top.

*"I'll just lay this half on top so we can all see where you cut the deck."*

**STEP 4:** Remove the crystal ball from your pocket, making sure the shell is snugly connected, and hold it up to the volunteer. It should be positioned so the volunteer can see the tiny card.

*"Gaze into my crystal ball. Look deep and tell me if you can see anything."*

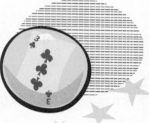

He should say, *"The three of clubs."* If he can't see anything, rotate the ball slightly to give him a head-on view.

*"Three of clubs? Really? You were supposed to see Dorothy. The three of clubs, huh? Hey...maybe that's the card you cut to."*

**STEP 5:** Pick up the top section of the cross cut and set it aside on the magic trunk. We know what you're thinking: That's not the card he cut to and the three of clubs is not in that pile! Shhh! Do you want to give it away?

*"Go ahead...look at the card you cut to. I dare you!"*

Point to the top card of the bottom section of the crosswise cut—that's the three of clubs! Because of the cross cut and the distraction of the crystal ball, you can be pretty certain the volunteer and the audience won't remember what card he really cut to. This little bit of misdirection, aided by your pointing finger, is a great way to fool everybody.

While he reaches for the top card, casually remove the plastic shell and slip it into your pocket. Place the ball on the table so anyone can inspect it and see that it's "ordinary."

**STEP 6:** The volunteer flips over the card and...by gosh, it's the three of clubs! But you already knew that, didn't you? That's why you're the magician!

HOMEWORK: Practice slipping the plastic shell on and off the ball so no one can see. Remember, when you're doing the trick, everyone will be staring at you like you've got three eyes, so you need to do this part quickly and without giving anything away.

EXTRA CREDIT: Mix it up a little! Have one volunteer gaze into the crystal ball while another reveals the cut card.

---

**WRISTY BUSINESS**

The German-born American mentalist Axel Vogt, whose stage name was Hellstrom, practiced a technique in the 1920s that became known as *hellstromism*. Also called *contact mind reading* or *muscle reading*, the magician performing the trick has a volunteer hide an object. Then the magician holds the volunteer's wrist and walks with him around the room or theater where the object is hidden. By paying attention to the tiny movements of the volunteer's wrist muscles, the magician can find the hidden object.

Hellstromism is a very tough trick to master, and only a very few magicians can do it. The American magician known as Kreskin has been using the technique to find his paycheck at performances since 1970. If he can't find it, he doesn't get paid!

# SOUL Catcher

**Lesson:** Capture the image of a card in the crystal ball!

## capture the moment

By using the plastic half shell and the tiny card glued inside, you can make it appear that you've captured the image of the card in your crystal ball.

## magic must-haves: Magic trunk

## from your mentalism kit: Crystal ball and shell, marked and tapered deck of cards (actually, any deck will do)

## extras: A volunteer who doesn't know the trick

## backstage

*Palm* (that is, hide) the plastic shell in your left hand and place the three of clubs at the top of the deck.

> **Trick Tip:** This trick works best with a few people, 'cause people who are sitting too far away won't be able to see the trick, and if too many people are gathered close to you, they'll be able to figure out how you did it.

## show time!

*"Did you ever hear about the belief that when your picture is taken, it steals your soul? I don't know if a camera works that way, but I know one thing that does: a crystal ball."*

**STEP 1:** Show the volunteer the crystal ball.

*"Don't look at it too long, or bye-bye, soul! Trust me...I know."* (You can do your best evil chuckle at this point, if you want.)

**STEP 2:** Place the deck on the magic trunk and ask the volunteer to flip over the top card. Would you look at that! The three of clubs! Now place the crystal ball over the card.

Have the volunteer gaze into the crystal ball with you and see the face of the card (the three of clubs) through the ball on the top of the deck. Slowly raise the ball, keeping it above the card. See how the image of three of clubs gets smaller? That's because of a whole bunch of science stuff about magnification and light refraction. Take a science class to learn more, we're only talking magic here!

*"See how the crystal ball is making the image smaller? It looks like the card is trapped right in the middle of the ball. Cool, huh? But don't look too long! I don't want you getting trapped in there as well."*

**STEP 3:** When the volunteer looks away, use this distraction to slip the plastic shell around the crystal ball. Hold the ball over the three of clubs card once more. The shell should be at the bottom of the ball.

*"Okay, this time I'm going to trap the card inside the crystal ball. Watch."*

---

**Trick Tip:** The volunteer and the audience should be on your left. If they sit on your right, they might see you slip the shell onto the crystal ball!

---

**STEP 4:** Have the volunteer look through the crystal ball once more. This time, he'll see the tiny three of clubs that's taped to the plastic shell, but he won't know that! And you better not tell! Slowly lift the ball away from the card, and then flip the three of clubs facedown on the deck. The image is still inside the crystal ball. It's trapped! Make sure your volunteer and the audience can see the image.

*"Would you look at that!"*

**STEP 5:** To make the vision disappear, toss the crystal ball in the air. Don't worry, the plastic shell will stick on. Just make sure you catch the ball when it comes back down. Grab the ball with your left hand and quickly transfer it to your right. When you do, remove the plastic shell with your left hand and palm it. Toss or bounce the ball to your volunteer. As everyone follows the ball, slide the plastic shell into your pocket.

*"Go ahead. Inspect it. But don't gaze at it too long or else you'll—oh, you know what'll happen."*

HOMEWORK: Practice placing the plastic shell on the ball and removing it. This can be tricky and needs to be done secretly. Your audience isn't going to be astonished by your magic if they realize they're gazing into a plastic shell instead of a mysterious crystal ball.

# sNake eyes #11

**pROject:** Know what number is on the face of a die that's been hidden inside two cups!

## what's iN the cup?

Can you see through solid objects? How about not-so-solid objects? Well, luckily for you, the lids on the two cups aren't quite as thick as they look. In fact, by allowing the die to rest against the red lid of the smaller cup, you can read the spots on the die through the lid!

## magic must-haves: Magic trunk

## from your mentalism kit: Large cup, small cup, and die

## extras: A volunteer who doesn't know the trick

## show time!

*"Did you know I'm banned from Las Vegas? It's true. It's not 'cause I'm underage. It's 'cause I'm too good. The casinos see me and they lock the doors. But I'll tell you a secret. It's not really skill—I always win because I can hear the dice."*

> **Trick Tip:** You don't need a lot of light for this trick, but if the room is too dark, it'll be difficult to see through the lid.

**STEP 1:** Take the two cups, both lids, and the die and place them on the magic trunk. Audiences love to touch and grope things, so go ahead, let them. This is their chance to see that the cups are cups, the lids are lids, and the die is really a rare substance found on the third moon of Jupiter. Well, maybe not.

*"To prove I can hear the die, I'm going to ask a volunteer to select a number on the die, not tell it or show it to me, and place it in the little cup so that the number faces up."*

**STEP 2:** To assure your audience that you're not cheating (don't worry, you'll be cheating them later), turn your back. Let the volunteer place the die in the little cup with the chosen number face up and pop the lid on top. Once she's done, turn around.

*"So the die is safely hidden?"*

**STEP 3:** Now you must get the die to rest against the red lid so you can see what spots are faceup. There's a few ways to do this. You can tell the audience that you're going to place the little cup inside the big cup upside down, and then use this opportunity to glance (we said *glance*, not stare) at the die resting against the red cap.

**Magician's view**

Another way is to tell the audience you need to listen to the die. *"They whisper, you know."* When you raise the cup to your ear, tilt it so the die slides against the red lid and casually glance (you know that we mean glance, not stare, right?) at the spots. You can even shake the cup, pretending you didn't believe they really put the die in there, then let the die rest against the lid and—you got it—glance at the spots.

No matter what method you choose, the point is to give yourself the opportunity to check out the die as it rests against the red lid.

**STEP 4:** Place the small cup upside down in the large cup and put the lid on top.

*"These two barriers can't keep me from hearing the die, but you can. I need silence, please!"*

**STEP 5:** You don't really need silence, but it adds drama. This is your chance to try out some nice acting. Pretend that you're really listening for the whispering die. Strain, tilt your head. Say to an audience member, **"Stop breathing so loud."** Have fun with it. Finally, announce the answer.

*"The die speaks! The number is [say the number of spots at the top of die]!*

Ask your volunteer to confirm the number. What a shock! You got it right! Even though everyone now knows you're correct, remove the small cup from the large one, and then reveal the die.

**HOMEWORK:** Practice looking at the die once it's in the small cup. Make sure you do it quickly and so naturally that no one will suspect.

**extra credit:** Did you know that opposing sides of all die always add up to seven? Go check it out, we'll wait. See? The one and six are on opposite sides. So are the two and five and the three and four.

This little bit of knowledge can add an extra twist to the trick. Not only will you be able to guess the number on the top of the die but on the bottom as well. When you glance at the die while it's resting against the lid, let's say you see four spots. That means the number on the bottom of the die is three. If you see two spots, the bottom number is five.

At the end of the trick you can announce the number on the bottom, too. If you do this, let the volunteer take out the die and show it to the audience. Twice the "wows!" with only one die!

## THAT'S DICEY!

Ever hear of a dice cup? A few cheaters are sorry they ever did. Throughout history, dice have been used in games of chance and betting. Well, you can *bet* that when it comes to gambling for money, someone will always find a way to cheat.

To prevent this, dice cups were created to cover the dice so no one could cheat. The cups were ribbed on the inside, so that the dice would turn as they fell out of the cup. This made it very tough to control how the dice would fall (a favorite technique of cheaters). But that didn't stop *dice sharps*. (Those are people who specialize in cheating with dice.) In the 1940s, these sneaky types created *slick cups*, which were smooth on the inside, allowing the dice sharps once again to control the dice roll.

When you perform magic tricks with dice, you can always use this bit of trivia to distract the audience while you work your own magic. And remember, *die* is the term for a single dice, although you could be forgiven for saying "douse" (like mice and mouse) if you "never say die!"

# a Nose for Color #12

**assignment:** Guess the color of a crayon without peeking!

## sniff your way to magic

Actually, you don't really smell anything, and hopefully no one smells you! Before you continue, check your fingernails. Been biting them lately? Hope not! You'll need one of them to do this trick. All you're doing is secretly marking your thumbnail with a piece of crayon. By secretly checking out the color on your thumbnail, you've figured out which crayon your volunteer selected!

**magic must-haves:** Magic trunk

**homemade magic:** Four crayons, all the same size but of different colors. The darker colors—blue, red, black, purple—will leave the best mark

**extras:** One volunteer. Make sure she can work under pressure as this lucky volunteer will actually be handing you a crayon!

## backstage

This trick is so easy, you don't have to do anything. (But you did remember the part about not biting your fingernails, right?)

## show time!

*"They say a dog can smell fear, a mom can smell a lie, and no one wants to smell my dirty socks. Well, I've spent every waking hour teaching myself how to smell color! Sound amazing? That's because...it is!"*

**STEP 1:** Hold up the crayons so the audience can see them. Wave them under your nose and take a deep sniff. Ah! All your favorites! Now lay them out on the magic trunk. Call up a volunteer from the audience.

*"To prove I can smell color, I'll just turn around and you place any one of the crayons in my hand."*

**STEP 2:** Turn your back to the audience and have your volunteer hand you a crayon. And don't drop it! Keep your hands behind your back.

*"I want you to do me one more favor. Take the other crayons and hide them so their smells don't interfere. Put them in your sock or hide them under your shirt. Just don't eat them. I'm performing this trick tomorrow."*

**STEP 3:** Once she's hidden the crayons, turn back to face the audience, but keep your hands (and the one crayon) behind your back, hidden from the audience's sight. As soon as no one can see your hands, take the point of the crayon and make a mark on one of your thumbnails.

*"Now I'm starting to smell the color. It's really strong! Could it be red? Or blue, maybe?"*

**STEP 4:** As you speak, bring your hand with the crayon mark to the front so you (and only you!) can see the mark on your nail. Fold your thumb down so it's hidden behind your palm and from the audience's view. Now wave your hand toward your nose like you're brushing the color scent under your sniffing nostrils.

*"Different colors smell different. I really have to get a good whiff."*

**STEP 5:** Your hand with the crayon should still be behind your back. With the hand that has the crayon mark in front of your face, you can easily sneak a glance at the mark and see what color it is. Since the hand is in front of your face, the audience shouldn't be able to see your thumb.

*"Ah, yes! A fine choice, indeed. Your color is [say the color on your thumbnail]."*

**STEP 6:** After you say the color of the crayon, bring out the crayon and show it to the surprised audience! (And don't forget to ask for all your crayons back after the trick is over—crayons don't grow on trees, y'know!)

> **Trick Tip:** You might think you're all thumbs, but your thumbnail works great for this trick. But you can use whichever nail is right for you!

**HOMEWORK:** Place the crayon behind your back and practice making a mark on your thumbnail. This should be as smooth and easy as if you do it every day! The mark doesn't have to be big—just big enough for you to tell what color it is.

---

## DEAD MAN TALKING

Dr. Henry Slade wasn't really a doctor. He was a *spiritualist,* someone who claimed he could help people to communicate with dead relatives. During his *séances*—the ritual spiritualists use when they're attempting to talk to dead people—in the late 1800s, messages from the dead would mysteriously appear on school slates (those are kind of like mini blackboards; kids used to write on them instead of paper).

When the slates were placed under a table, they were blank. The lights were turned out for a few moments; when the lights were turned back on, there was writing on the slates! Years later, Slade admitted he was a fake, and demonstrated how he could remove his shoes, pick up a piece of chalk with his toes, and write messages faster than most people can write with their hands!

**exercise:** Find the "spy" hidden on a piece of paper!

## the spy catcher

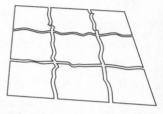

The success of this trick totally depends on your ability to tear a piece of paper into nine squares. It's a simple mentalism trick, but you really have to pay attention to which square of paper has four ragged sides. Some have two ragged sides, some have three, but only one has four—and that's the key to the whole thing.

## magic must-haves: Magic trunk

## homemade magic: Nine pencils and a sheet of letter-size paper, preferably not a sheet of looseleaf paper, 'cause the holes just get in the way.

## extras: Nine volunteers! You heard right—nine! What?! You don't have nine? Okay, fewer will work, but start playing to bigger audiences!

---

**Trick Tip:** You can use fewer than nine people for this trick, but we really recommend the whole nine. It'll prove that you really *do* have more friends than we do, and it makes this trick so much easier! (See, nine pieces of paper, nine people in the audience. It's genius!)

---

## backstage

Take the sheet of paper and tear it into nine fairly equal pieces. Don't cut it! To make the tearing easy, tear the paper into three equal strips and then tear each of those strips into three pieces.

# SHOW time!

*"I love magic, but it's really just a stepping-stone to what I really want to do: become an international man of danger and mystery. No, not a PE teacher. A spy! I've been reading all my secret spy manuals and they say one of the first skills a spy-in-training has to learn is how to catch another spy."*

**STEP 1:** Hand out a pencil and a torn piece of paper to each of your volunteers. There are eight regular pieces—those that have three or fewer ragged sides—and only one special piece. That's the piece that was at the center of your sheet of paper, the one with all four ragged sides.

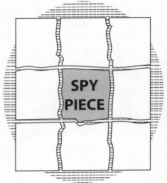

SPY PIECE

*"That's where you come in. You can help me in my spy training. I want each of you to come up here, one at a time, with your piece of paper, and I will tell you whether you are one of the eight helpless victims or the spy that I'm going to catch."*

**STEP 2:** Have each volunteer come up to you. Identify everyone who got a regular piece as a *"helpless victim."* Identify the person who got the ragged four-sided piece as the *"spy."*

**STEP 3:** Turn your back on your volunteers and cover your eyes.

*"If I identified you as a helpless victim, take the piece of paper I gave you and write down the type of secret government document or valuable you're trying to protect from the spy. If I identified you as the spy, write down your evil spy code name. I suggest something like Mr. Evil or Vlad the Not-So-Nice."*

**STEP 4:** While you still have your back turned to the audience, ask for one of the volunteers to do this favor for you.

"Collect all of the pieces of paper, please, and lay them facedown on the magic trunk. Put them in any order, but don't let any of them touch. These spies are tricky!"

**STEP 5**: Turn around. By looking at the nine pieces of paper, you can tell the ragged four-sided piece from the others. If you can't, then you've torn the pieces poorly (or your friends are trying to trick you)!

"I'm going to identify which of these pieces of paper belongs to the spy. But I have to be careful. If I pick a helpless victim, then the spy'll steal something important and get away!"

**STEP 6**: Pick up the ragged square and flip it over. Read the name of the spy.

"Aha! I've caught you, Vlad the Not-So-Nice [or whatever name the spy wrote down]! I told you I'd catch him!"

**HOMEWORK**: Practice tearing the paper evenly! You want all nine squares to be about the same size.

---

### NOT SEEING IS BELIEVING

Washington Irving Bishop, a 19th-century American mentalist who called himself "The First and World Eminent Mind Reader" was the first magician to perform the *blindfold drive*. Securely blindfolded, he drove a horse and carriage through the streets without causing an accident!

Another favorite routine of his was to conduct a pretend murder. While he stepped out of the room, the audience would pick a murderer, a weapon, and a victim. When he returned he would "psychically" figure out all three.

**PROJECT:** Predict the name of a United States president that a volunteer randomly pulls out of a bag!

## HAIL TO THE CHIEF

Too young to vote? Doesn't matter! With this trick you get to pick a U.S. president. Actually, you're just predicting the name a volunteer will pull out of a bag. What the audience doesn't know is that all the names in the bag are the *same*, so you can't be wrong!

**MAGIC MUST-HAVES:** Magic trunk

**HOMEMADE MAGIC:** Small pieces of paper you can fit in your hand, a pencil, and a paper bag

**EXTRAS:** A bunch of volunteers—at least six

> **Trick Tip:** You can use cut-up index cards or sticky notes instead of small pieces of paper. Just make sure they're small enough for you to write on while holding them in your palm.

## BACKSTAGE

Just practice your killer smile.

## SHOW TIME!

*"I'm too young to vote. Sure, it's hard to believe, but it's true. But even though I can't go to the polls, I'm going to pick the president of the United States that you're thinking of. And I'm going to pick him out of a bag—but that doesn't mean he's tiny."*

**STEP 1:** Show the audience that the bag is empty. And to prove it's solid, have one of them wear it. It's not necessary, but it sure makes them look funny! Take the small pieces of paper and pencil and prepare to write down the name of a U.S. president. Now pick a volunteer from the audience and have him say the name of any president, past or present.

**STEP 2:** Okay, now this is where the lying—we mean magic—comes in. Let's say your first volunteer says **George Washington**. You know him. Father of the country. Chopped down a cherry tree. All that stuff. Well, when he says **George Washington**, you repeat the name, but you write **Abe Lincoln** on the note. No, you don't do this because you can't spell George. You'll see why later. Just make sure no one sees what you really write; quickly fold the note in half, and drop it in the bag.

**STEP 3:** Next! Move to another volunteer and have her say the name of another president. This time, the volunteer says **Thomas Jefferson**. You repeat the president's name, but write down...you guessed it...**Abe Lincoln**. Quickly fold up this note, and toss it in the bag, too.

**STEP 4:** Simply repeat Steps 2 and 3. Ask another volunteer to name yet another president. No matter what name the volunteer picks, you repeat the name of the president but write down **Abe Lincoln**. Quickly fold up this piece and toss it in the bag. Continue to ask for names and write **Abe Lincoln** on every note until someone finally says **Abe Lincoln**. It's very important that you continue to get names until someone finally says the one you've been writing down on the notes.

**STEP 5:** Once someone finally says **Abe Lincoln** (or whatever president you've selected to write down on all the notes), gather a few more names, continuing to write **Abe Lincoln** on each, then stop. It's always best to get six or more presidents in the bag—that really makes the trick freaky.

> **Trick Tip:** You can do this trick with any number of volunteers, but it's best to have at least six. Just make sure you keep asking the audience to feed you names until someone finally calls out the president you kept writing on the notes! Make sure that you pick a really common one. Can you really depend on your audience to pick Millard Fillmore?

*"Okay. I think that's enough presidents in one bag, don't you? Like I said, I'm too young to vote, but I'm still going to pick the president!"*

**STEP 6:** Hold the bag in your hand and ask a volunteer (it can be one of the people who "voted") to pick one note and hold on to it. Make sure he only picks one, otherwise you'll be wearing the bag (courtesy of an angry audience) when this trick ends. Once he picks the single note, take the bag away and put it out of sight. We don't want any snoops digging up more Lincolns.

*"Now get ready. I'm going to use my amazing powers of vote-ocity to tell you which president you picked."*

At this point wave your hands around above your head, grit your teeth, make a big show, as if you're really concentrating. Why? People love a show! Then stop.

*"Aaannnddd... the winner of this election is... Abe Lincoln!"*

**STEP 7:** Have the volunteer unfold the paper and show everyone...Abe Lincoln!

*"Now if you want to see a real trick, I'll try to explain the Electoral College."*

HOMEWORK: The key to this trick is making the audience really believe you're writing down the names they're calling out. If you toss in some trivia about the presidents they chose while you're writing down **Abe Lincoln** (or whatever president *you* choose), it will make a better illusion. So go hit your history books! Now, that's some *real* homework. Sorry.

Here are some facts to get you started:

1. **Lyndon Johnson:** He took the oath of office on an airplane!

2. **Andrew Jackson:** His portrait is on the twenty-dollar bill.

3. **Ronald Reagan:** The only president who was also a movie star!

---

**DEAD LETTER OFFICE**

The idea of magically reading unseen information that has been written on a small piece of paper was invented by Charles H. Foster, a Massachusetts mentalist who practiced his tricks in the mid-1800s. He would have his clients write the names and some characteristics of a dead relative on a piece of paper and fold it up so no one could see what was written. Then Mr. Foster would magically reveal the name and other information about the deceased.

# X-RAY eyes #15

**LeSSON:** Without peeking, guess what color ball an audience member has pulled out of a bag!

## HOLeY papeR BaGS!

What good *is* a bag with a hole in the side? Well, it's *no* good! Unless you're doing magic. By using a gimmicked bag that has a hole cut in it, you're able to see what color ball an audience member has pulled out and is hiding in his palm.

## maGic muSt-HaveS: Magic trunk

## HomemaDe maGic: Here's the long list, so get

ready! A lunch bag, cellophane or plastic wrap, clear tape, scissors, and four pieces of colored paper: one green, one yellow, one blue, and one red

## extraS: One volunteer capable of reaching into a bag;

one audience capable of gasping in amazement

## BackstaGe

Lots to do here, so maybe you should take a day off from school to get ready (although we can't imagine the excuse note your folks will write for you). First, use the scissors to cut a two-inch-by-four-inch window in the back of the lunch bag, toward the bottom. Now leave this bag in the cupboard for your brother to use for school the next day. Well, actually, no. This is the bag you'll use for the trick. Now cut a piece of cellophane or plastic wrap slightly bigger than the window in the brown bag. Tape time! Tape the cellophane or plastic wrap to the

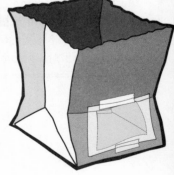

inside of the bag so that the cellophane or plastic wrap covers the window. Here comes the really hard part. Take the four pieces of colored paper and crumple them up into balls. Oh, wait, that wasn't hard at all. Drop the colored paper balls into the bag and fold up the bag so the window is hidden.

## SHOW time!

*"You know what happens when you watch too much TV? You see a lot of bad TV shows, that's what. But a second thing happens that not too many people are aware of. You get X-ray vision."*

**STEP 1:** Take the bag and unfold it. Make sure the window in the bag faces you and that no one else can see it! Place the bag on the table and remove the four colored paper balls. Place these on the trunk, next to the bag.

*"I have four balls in different colors. And in case one of you is missing four pieces of colored paper...I didn't take them!"*

**STEP 2:** Take the four balls and drop them into the bag, one at a time. With your left hand, hold the bag at eye-level. Make sure the window is hidden from the audience! Now, get a volunteer from the audience.

*"To prove I have X-ray vision, I'm going to have you pick any ball from the bag. Then I will use my X-ray eyes to cut through your very flesh so I can see the ball hidden in your hand. Don't worry! It won't hurt...much."*

**STEP 3:** Turn your head away (audiences love it when you turn your head away) and have your volunteer reach into the bag and pull out a paper ball.

> **Trick Tip:** Make sure you keep the cellophane or plastic wrap window at your eye level. This not only makes it easier to take a peek, but holding the bag high will prevent any snoopy volunteer from looking inside and seeing the window.

*"Grab a ball. They don't bite! Make sure you hide it from me."*

**STEP 4:** When the volunteer tells you the ball is safely hidden behind his back or in his hand, turn back around. Make sure you don't look at the bag yet. If you stare directly into the window, it may tip people off.

*"Now, you may feel your hand tingle a little bit. Don't worry! That's just my X-ray eyes peeking through your flesh to see what color you took from the bag."*

> **Trick Tip:** It's important that the audience sees that you're not peeking. So turn your head, cover your eyes, do anything you want, just make sure they have no doubt that the ball's color is hidden from you...and your X-ray eyes!

**STEP 5:** Use the words *"took from the bag"* as a diversion to naturally look at the cellophane window. It's important to glance at it long enough to see what color ball is missing. For example, if you see a green, a yellow, and a red paper ball inside the bag, you know the volunteer took the blue one. Don't stare at the bag like it's a three-headed chicken! You don't want the audience to guess there's something fishy about that bag.

*"I need to really focus here. If my X-ray vision misfires, who knows what horrible tattoos I may see hidden under your clothes.. Okay...I see your bones, blood looks good, and there's a...a...hmmm...you might want to have a doctor look at that bruise. And...yes! I see the ball. It's the color [name the color he's holding].*

**STEP 6:** The audience will certainly think this is the most amazing thing they've seen since Uncle Fred ate an entire tub of potato salad by himself, and they'll plead with you to do it again. No, not to eat an entire tub of potato salad but to use your X-ray vision. Luckily, this is one of those rare tricks that you can do a second time.

*"I can tell you're all amazed. Sometimes I even amaze myself! And since you're such a fine audience, I guess I can show you the trick once more."*

Have the volunteer place the paper ball he chose on the magic trunk, and then ask him to pick a new ball from the bag. But before he does so, tell him that he shouldn't let anyone see the new paper ball; in fact, *he* shouldn't even look at it!

*"If you don't know what color the ball is, either, this will stop me from doing something easy...like reading your mind."*

Repeat steps 3 through 5, and name the color of the ball in the volunteer's hand. Once you do, have the volunteer show the audience (and himself!) which ball he holds. Look at that! You got it right again! Wow! Even *we're* starting to believe you have X-ray eyes.

*"I'll let you in on a little secret. The first time, I didn't use my X-ray vision at all. I just read your mind. But this time, it was all X-ray. Now I want to make things a little difficult. The only thing that can stop my X-ray eyes is lead, so if I could borrow a solid lead glove from anyone in the audience, I can do something really amazing."*

**STEP 7:** Unless one of your friends is really weird, odds are no one will have a lead glove with them.

*"Hmm, so much for that trick. But I've got another idea."*

Have the volunteer take one of the last two balls from the bag while you turn your head. After he takes one of the balls, check the window in the bag to see which color it is, just like you did in step 5. Ask him to hold that ball high above his head, squeezed in his hand so that no one can see the ball. Now have the volunteer use his free hand to pull out the second ball. Ask him to hold this ball high above his head as well. You won't need to check the window this time, because there were only two colors left! Once he pulls out his hand, casually fold up the paper bag and put it away. Make sure you do this casually enough that no one suspects the bag may be special.

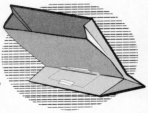

*"Okay, this is going to be tricky because I'm going to try to see both balls at once."*

Now squint one eye, then the other. Scratch your head. Get some drama going! If you ever wanted to be an actor, now's the time to put on a little show.

*"I see a [name color] ball in your left hand and a [name color] ball in your right!"*

Have the volunteer show the audience and just sit back and soak up the applause.

HOMEWORK: Practice glancing through the cellophane or plastic wrap window so it's almost unnoticeable. This is the key to making this trick really mysterious. If you can do it without the audience catching on, you'll really amaze them!

---

## THEY COULDN'T SEE THROUGH *THIS* TRICK

Only Superman has X-ray vision, right? Some magicians think that real-life magician Kuda Bux had it, too. He was born in Pakistan and developed the best *X-ray Eye* act in show business. He used a very complex blindfolding technique consisting of bread dough, cotton pads, gauze, and heavy napkins, all wrapped over his face and head to prevent any light from entering his eyes. Despite the blindfold, he was able to copy words written on a chalkboard and ID objects that audience members took from their pockets.

Many magicians claimed they knew how Kuda Bux did it, but since he died in 1981, no one has duplicated his uncanny act. But here's the most amazing thing: In the last years of his life, his vision began to fail and he was declared legally blind. Despite this handicap, he was *still* able to do his *Sightless Vision* routine.

**project:** Predict a word that a volunteer will say!

## it's a know-know

This is a fun and humorous trick that won't leave your audience amazed, but it will leave them laughing. All you do is write the word **NO** on a piece of cardboard, then ask a volunteer if he knows the hidden word. Naturally, he'll say no and he'll be right!

**homemade magic:** A piece of cardboard and a marker

**extras:** One audience and one person in the audience capable of speaking

## backstage

Take the piece of cardboard and write the word **NO** on it in really large letters. That's it. Oh, wait! Fold it in half. *Now* you're done.

## show time!

*"Everyone can read minds, right?"* Look for someone shaking their head no and add, *"Well, except for you."*

**STEP 1:** Pull out the folded piece of cardboard, and unfold it but don't let the audience see that you've written something on it already. Take the marker and pretend to write a word.

*"One thing that I find harder than eating broccoli is to project my thoughts. But I've been practicing lately. I'm going to write down a word and then project it to one of you."*

**STEP 2:** Fold the cardboard in half and pick a volunteer.

*"Word written. Mind projecting. Sending the image. Okay! Do you know the word I wrote down?"*

Obviously he doesn't and will answer, **"No."**

**STEP 3:** Amazing! Unfold the cardboard and reveal the word **NO**.

*"Wow! That was easier than I thought."*

extra credit: You can throw the audience a little curveball by using the homonym **KNOW** instead of **NO**.

homework: Hmmm. Not much. Maybe practice writing the word **NO** so it's nice and neat. Or better yet, work on folding and unfolding the cardboard. That's really fun!

## MUM'S THE WORD

Jean Robert-Houdin, who is today considered the father of modern magic, was known for his feature *Second Sight* in his magic show. Robert-Houdin would enter the audience and borrow objects from them. Meanwhile, his son, Emile, would stand blindfolded on the stage and say what items Robert-Houdin was borrowing from an audience member. Whether it was jewelry, handkerchiefs, coins, watches, or other objects, Emile always seemed to guess correctly! Their secret? Father and son had created a complicated verbal code that created the illusion that Emile was clairvoyant. It was with this act that Robert-Houdin became, in 1846, a huge success at the Soirées Fantastiques, a small theater in Paris.

# animal iNstiNct #17

**exercise:** Predict which four-legged animal a volunteer will name!

## olò macòonalò haò a farm

This is another fun trick that's good for a laugh. All you need to do is draw a silly four-legged animal that could look like any animal. You don't actually predict anything. Your drawing looks so general, it could be any animal!

**homemaòe magic:** A piece of cardboard and a marker pen

**extras:** One audience that knows the difference between a two-legged and a four-legged animal and one volunteer

## backstage

Nothing to do but make animal noises.

## show time!

*"I love drawing. It's my second favorite hobby (after magic, of course). But I can do something really weird. Not only can I draw an animal from my head, I can draw one from any of yours as well."*

**STEP 1:** Pick a volunteer and have her think of a four-legged farm animal but not tell you what it is.

**STEP 2:** Take the marker pen and the piece of cardboard and draw a basic, silly, four-legged animal. No art skills? Good! The sillier the animal looks, the better.

*"I'm getting an oinkage. It's moooo-ving into my head. I'll draw it on the baaa-baaack of the cardboard. Just a ruff! drawing."*

**STEP 3:** Ask the volunteer to tell everyone the four-legged farm animal she was thinking of. No matter what animal she says, you spin your card around and show your drawing.

*"It's purrrrrfect!"*

> **Trick Tip:** The picture should be general enough that it can be any four-legged farm animal, including a dog, cow, horse, pig, cat, etc.

HOMEWORK: If you really want to get laughs, practice animal noises to make while you draw the animal.

---

## PSYCHIC BUSTER

James Randi, also known as the Amazing Randi, first became famous as a fantastic, Houdini-like escape artist, performing feats like escaping from a straitjacket while hanging over Niagara Falls! Nowadays, he spends his time working with **CSICOPS**, the Committee for the Scientific Investigation of Claims of the Paranormal, a group of magicians and scientists who investigate people who claim to have psychic abilities such as talking to the dead, healing the sick through the power of touch, moving objects just by thinking about them, and more.

He has exposed lots of these false psychics, who use classic magician's techniques to convince innocent people of their marvelous mental powers. If these fakers have any magic at all, it's in their skill for making their victims' money disappear (when they charge for their services).

# Numbers Game #18

**assignment:** Predict a number that a volunteer is thinking of!

## three's a crowd

Are you a risk-taker? This trick isn't as risky as bungee jumping, but for a magician, it sure comes close! After you write down the number three on a piece of paper, ask a volunteer to pick a number between one and four. Most people pick three, which is the number you wrote down! What's that? You'd rather bungee jump than take the risk? Then move on to the next trick.

**magic must-haves:** Magic trunk

**homemade magic:** A piece of cardboard or paper and a pen

**extras:** One volunteer. Hopefully, his favorite number is three.

## backstage

Write the numbers 1, 2, 3, and 4 on a piece of cardboard or paper. On the back of this paper, write the number 3.

> **Trick Tip:** Make sure the 3 written on the back can't be seen through the writing material once you flip it over. For this reason, cardboard always works well.

# SHOW time!

*"I actually learned this trick from my mom. She can always tell exactly what I'm thinking just by looking at my face."*

**STEP 1:** Select a volunteer. Anyone wearing a T-shirt that says "I love the number three" should be your immediate choice. Pull out the paper with the numbers. Place it on the magic trunk with the 1,2,3, 4 side face-up. Make sure no one can see the 3 on the back side!

*"When I snap my fingers, I want you to pick any one of these numbers."*

**STEP 2:** Stare at the volunteer's face. Look into his eyes, inspect his chin, check out his nose. Make it really look like you're reading his face. Then, snap your fingers.

At this point your volunteer should say three. Why? Most people pick three. We don't know why, it's just something a bunch of goofball scientists figured out.

**Trick Tip:** What if the volunteer doesn't say three? Well, you could get a new volunteer, but it would be best if you used the goof to segue into a new trick. For example, if he says one, reply *"That's right. One. Now I'm going to show you one amazing trick."* Then begin the *X-ray Eyes* trick. Or if he says two, reply *"As in second. And the second President of the United States was John Adams."* Then begin the *Presidential Bag* trick. The point is to cover up! The audience may not understand why you did all that, but it sure is better than having them realize the trick didn't work.

**STEP 3:** Once he says three, flip over the piece of paper and reveal the three you already wrote.

*"Do me a favor. Make sure you never try to lie to my mom."*

HOMEWORK: Practice what you'll do if the trick doesn't work. The rest of the trick is easy as pie, so work on a way to get out of the trick if the volunteer doesn't pick three!

# a WORD to the WiSe
ephc #19

**exercise:** Predict the word the audience will choose from a book!

## ReaDiNG is fuNDameNTaL

If you can count and read, this trick is a breeze. If you can't count and read, then you won't be able to read this sentence telling you this trick should be impossible to do! A volunteer picks a page and counts to, let's say, the twenty-first word on that page. By using a duplicate book hidden from the audience, you can figure out what word the volunteer will choose.

**magic musT-Haves:** Magic trunk

**HomemaDe magic:**
Two copies of the same book

**exTRas:** A volunteer who can read and an audience of at least two others.

> **Trick Tip:** This trick can also be done with duplicate newspapers, magazines, and even comic books!

## BacksTage

Nothing to do but catch up on your reading—and hide one copy of the book in the next room.

## SHOW time!

*"I love to read. I read books, magazines, cereal boxes, mouthwash ingredients. In fact, I love reading so much, I've memorized every word in this book."*

**STEP 1:** Hold up the other copy of the book—the one you didn't hide.

*"This book has all my favorite words: 'the,' 'it,' 'they,' 'onomatopoeia.' But to prove I've memorized every word on every page of this book, I'll let you chose the page and word, and I'll guess what it is. I hope you choose 'molasses.' That's a good one."*

**STEP 2:** Hand the book to someone in the audience, and make sure it's someone who can read. This trick won't work very well if the person stares at the words and drools. It'll also ruin your book.

*"Now I need two more volunteers. My dad wants me to pull weeds in the garden and I don't want to do it alone. No takers? Okay, then how about just picking two numbers?"*

**STEP 3:** Ask the volunteer to tell everyone how many pages are in the book. Let's say 300. Now ask the first volunteer to pick a number between 1 and 300. The second volunteer should pick a number between 1 and 20. For our example, let's go with 203 and 15.

*"I want you [point to the volunteer with the book] to turn to page 203 and count down to the fifteenth word. Tell the rest of the audience that word, once I've stepped out of the room to make sure I have no way of hearing."*

**STEP 4:** Leave the room.

*"Toodles!"*

**STEP 5:** This is where the counting comes in. Take the second copy of the book you have hidden away and quickly turn to page 203 and count to the fifteenth word. Let's say it's *telephone*.

203

Nau malbela bieroj bele skribas kvin auxtoj. Multaj katoj acx la tre bona vojo. **Telephone** igxis du malbona bildoj. Kvar belega domoj veturas, kaj Ludviko romenos. Nau stulta auxtoj malvarme pripensis tri vere eta katoj. La radioj malbele igxis tri cxambroj, sed ses tratoj kuris, kaj kvar bieroj havas kvin auxtoj. Kvar flava katoj gajnas tri tre rapida auxtoj. Ses malbona libroj saltas, sed kvin birdoj blinde skribas ses vere malbela arboj, kaj Londono havas kvar birdoj, sed multaj flava vojoj acxetis du alrapida kalkuliloj, kaj cxambroj pripensis ses flava arboj. Multaj alrapida hundoj gajnas

**STEP 6:** Return to the room with your audience, but be sure to hide your copy of the book first! Don't take it with you or let anyone see it. Hide it under a bed or behind the dresser, or whatever—just get rid of the evidence!

"Did you find the word? Good. It's not as cool as 'molasses,' but it'll do. The fifteenth word on the two hundred and third page is...oh...excuse me...I have to go answer the TELEPHONE. I'll be right back!"

---

**Trick Tip:** To make sure the audience counts correctly, set up some rules. Yes, "a," "the," and "it" count as words. Hyphenated words like "no-show" count as one word and partial words count as one. "I have a tremen—what's that!?" would be six words even though "tremendous" is cut short. Finally, contractions like "what's," don't," and "isn't" are also one word. This explanation may seem unnecessary, but it assures everyone counts the same way!

---

HOMEWORK: Find two matching books and if you're really up for an amazing trick, really memorize every word. (Ha, ha.) The easier homework would be to practice counting words so you can be quick and, most of all, accurate.

---

## REMOTE-CONTROL READING

The jet-black hair, sinister-looking goatee, and arched eyebrows of Max Maven make him look pretty spooky—and he is! Max Maven has read more minds than anyone in history. That's because he's made more television appearances than any mentalist in recent times, reading the minds of the audiences at home with his special interactive mind–reading routines.

He does some amazing things in his show. He lets a volunteer decide how a newspaper will be torn into smaller and smaller pieces until only one piece is left, and on that piece is the very word he predicted!

If you ask Max if he really reads minds, he'll explain, "I use psychology, body language, and intuition. That's why I say, 'Always remember to think good thoughts—you never know who might be listening!'"

# ONe of a KiNd #20

## Lesson: Find the card in a deck of fifty-two!

### two-faced

Finding a card is so very easy, especially when you've gimmicked the deck by creating a two-sided card!

### magic must-haves: Magic trunk

### Homemade magic: Glue or rubber cement, a deck of fifty-two cards, one duplicate card from another deck, a pencil, an envelope and a piece of paper

### Backstage

Get ready to gimmick! Take one card from a second deck and find its duplicate in your deck. Glue the backs together so that the same face appears on both sides.

Once everything has dried, take your special card and slide it back into your regular deck. Now place the deck on the magic trunk along with your pencil, envelope, and piece of paper.

> **TRICK TIP:** Spread the glue evenly on the card backs. You want the cards to stick together without any wrinkling or bubbles so that it really looks like just one card when you're done. You can also press the cards between two heavy books to flatten them.

## SHOW time!

*"My uncle once tried to play a stupid card game with me called Fifty-two-Card Pickup. He threw the cards in the air and said: 'There're the fifty-two cards. Pick 'em up.' Ha. Ha. But I figured out a way to get back at him."*

**STEP 1:** Hold up your deck of cards to the audience.

*"I went to my uncle and asked him to play Fifty-two-Card Pickup with me again. He was all over it and he took the cards from me."*

**STEP 2:** Grab the pencil and piece of paper and write down the name of the card that you gimmicked—the double-face card.

*"Before he started, I wrote down something secret on a piece of paper and sealed it in an envelope."*

**STEP 3:** Stick the piece of paper in the envelope and seal it shut—lick it carefully so you don't cut your tongue. We don't have a magic trick to repair tongues!

*"He wanted to know what I was doing and I said I knew which card would be left faceup at the end of the game."*

**STEP 4:** Hand the envelope to someone in the audience. Pick up the cards from the magic trunk and throw them in the air.

*"He laughed. He didn't believe me. I knew I had him."*

**STEP 5:** When they fall to the ground, pick up the facedown cards, square them up, and put them facedown on the magic trunk.

*"He laughed some more and pointed out that lots of cards were faceup."*

**STEP 6:** Now pick up all the faceup cards, square them up, and hold them in your hands.

*"And I told him I wasn't done yet."*

**STEP 7:** Throw the cards in the air again. After they land, pick up the facedown cards and place them with the other facedown cards on the magic trunk. Then pick up all the faceup cards and hold them in your hand.

*"By this time, he was thinking he'd suckered me again—all I was doing was throwing cards in the air and picking them up again. But I had him totally fooled—I knew exactly what I was doing."*

**STEP 8:** Repeat Step 7 again and again until only one card lands faceup.

*"So he kept smiling and I kept throwing the cards in the air!"*

**STEP 9:** That one card is your secret double-face card that's been landing faceup the whole time, only now it's the only one left.

*"'Game over,' I told him. He wasn't impressed until I had him open the sealed envelope."*

**STEP 10:** Ask your volunteer to open the envelope and read the name of the card written on the piece of paper. It should match the only card on the floor.

*"Now my uncle's so impressed he won't try any more card tricks on me."*

JACK
OF
HEARTS

**HOMEWORK:** Throwing cards in the air and watching them fly around is lots of fun, but you want to do it carefully. If you throw them wildly, you look like some nut who likes to throw cards. And if you're too wild, you risk losing your secret double-face card. And this is not a trick you want to repeat for the same audience—your double-face card will come up again and they'll get very suspicious!

# CONCLUSiON

Great job mastering mentalism! You now have three Magic University courses in your head—Transformations, Illusions, and Mentalism—and you're getting closer to being a bona fide magician!

Mentalism has taught you how to create magic of the mind. You can now make your friends believe that you have ESP as you demonstrate your extraordinary senses of touch, sight, and hearing. You can use duplicate writing to predict an election. You can use psychological preferences to correctly guess numbers and colors. And when your family and friends think this is all just too amazing, there are a couple of mind-reading comedy tricks to get them laughing.

If your mind is tired from all this mentalism, we don't blame you—ours get tired too. But the brain is a muscle and it needs regular exercise. There's no better way to do that than by practicing your mentalism magic.

Next month, a whole new set of tricks will *appear*—'cause next month's topic is Appearing and Disappearing!

# about magicians JOHN RaiLiNG aNd DaNNY ORLeaNS

There's more to magic than just doing tricks. This month at Magic University, our two guest professors are busy even when they don't have a deck of cards in their hands.

You don't think of a lawyer doing magic, but that's what **John Railing** is! He started performing magic tricks professionally while he was in law school and soon became one of the country's top *close-up* magicians. A close-up magician specializes in sleight-of-hand tricks that include cards, coins, balls, and a bunch of great (and weird) mental tricks.

From the Windy City of Chicago, he performs for celebrities, entertainers, and leading corporate executives. He has also performed for presidents, foreign dignitaries, and heads of state from around the world.

John consults and produces magic tricks and toys. He's currently working with David Copperfield to develop toys, games, books, magic tricks, and even restaurants and stores!

Our second guest professor is **Danny Orleans**. Remember when we told you you're never too young to start thinking about magic? Well, Danny has wanted to be a magician since he was six years old. Raised in suburban Livingston, New Jersey, Danny performed professionally as a teenager and had his own one-man magic show in college.

After college, Danny developed educational magic to teach nutrition, math, human perception, and the meaning of friendship to children. With his family magic, he performs regularly at children's events, hospitals, and at corporate family functions, conventions, and festivals. He also writes articles for magic magazines like *The Linking Ring* and *Genii*.

# WHat's NeW witH tom maſon aNd DaN DaNko

## Tom Mason

Here's another fun and amazing fact about Tom that you didn't already know: His favorite movie is in black and white. He just can't remember what it's called.

## Dan Danko

Here's something you didn't know about Dan: He's currently writing a new video game that's so secret, he doesn't know the name of it and has to write code while blindfolded!